# SEEN BUT NOT HEARD

A True Story of Survival & Hope

# Seen But Not Heard

## A True Story of Survival & Hope

JANET LINTON

StoryTerrace

# CONTENTS

# TRIGGER WARNING

Dear reader,
This is not just a book about overcoming childhood trauma ...

My story explores the damage done to the psyche of a child who was abused by the adults who should have cared for her. It will reveal the moments that shaped my behaviour as a young person, the effects that those moments had on my relationships with friends and family and the consequences I live with to this day, as an adult.

My story is also one of triumph. I have worked hard to break down barriers, both within and without. I have dedicated my career to helping others find strength within themselves, and I will continue to help my clients foster their own well-being and build resilience. Ultimately, I have discovered the true meaning of love and found the strength within to break the cycle of abuse that scars my family history to this day.

Please be aware that some of the topics in this book may be uncomfortable to read. If you have experienced any kind of abuse or trauma, please ensure you read this book with open eyes in a safe space and that you have your support network engaged. If you can, persevere with me till the end and see how my life has changed and is still transforming today. Stay with me as I take my life into my own hands, plant my feet and bloom and hopefully, you will see the light at the end of the tunnel too.

Please visit www.supportline.org.uk for information or support for adult survivors of childhood abuse, if you're in the UK, or www.ascasupport.org if you're in the US.

# 1

## MY EARLY YEARS

*'Family is supposed to be our safe haven. Very often, it's the place where we find our deepest heartache.'*

–Iyanla Vanzant

I was born in the industrial town of Walsall, the town of a hundred trades and an offshoot of Birmingham, the city of a thousand, in 1988. Born under the summer sun, I was a true Cancerian: generous and clever, determined and focused, and with an enduring innocence. Apparently, July babies are more optimistic than most, and I wonder if it's this characteristic that has been my saviour over the years, keeping me going, urging me on . . .

And so I was thrust into a charismatic clash of cultures. For all intents and purposes, my home was just like everyone else's, (Black Country brick and mortar), but on the inside, the strict Jamaican heritage and Trinidadian calypso cultures jumped the gaps in the oceans and fed into my growing soul.

Dad, a Jamaican native, was 20 years older than Mom; she was 16 when they first met. Unfortunately, I don't remember anything about him, him having passed before I'd reached the age of three and sadly, there's no one to ask because it's not talked about in our world. On my dad's death certificate, I learned he was born in Jamaica in 1939, worked with asbestos and died in the UK of a heart attack in 1990.

Mom and Dad had four kids together in all, though it wasn't until I'd reached adulthood that I was to find out about their first-born child, W, who they'd had when Mom turned 18, I'm guessing and then lost to cot death as an infant. I have an older brother, D, who I've grown up with and a younger sister, Mel, who has a different dad to me and D.

I've also come to learn that I have more siblings than I thought; I've since met brothers M, E, and H and sister, S, but given my family's reluctance to talk about my dad, I'm just not sure how many half-siblings and distant relatives I might have out there. As I've grown, I've come to terms with the fact that we're not all going to sit around the dinner table together, comparing childhood stories; mine are too dark anyway.

Mom had always worked hard from a young age; that's without question. I do question though, if, at such a young age (16), she'd suffocated under the strictness of her relationship with my dad and wonder if this might have had an impact on the way she parented me.

What I do know is that when I started school in 1992, my Mom worked full-time at a factory. Unfortunately, work seemingly came before everything else, which I didn't quite understand as she was raising us single-handedly, but, as school wouldn't open early enough and would then cast us out at the stroke of three, that meant we'd have to have before- and after-school care, which began at my nan's.

Nan lived a short distance from school, so we'd go in the mornings, returning at the end of the school day, until Mom picked us up for home and bed. It was Mother's Day 1993 when we lost her. I remember being at Nan's funeral, watching this long box be lowered into the ground, feeling confused at Mom's and all the other adults' tears, not understanding what it all meant, not comprehending she'd gone forever.

Of course, life returned to normal, but we still needed care, and so it was agreed we'd go to my auntie's, (Nan's sister), who lived just over the road from Nan's old house. At that time, I'd discovered a love of athletics and sports in general, and I was good! Everyone seemed to love me back then as I won medals for running, netball and basketball. Life didn't seem so bad; it's a real shame it didn't last.

*My brother and me*

*Me*

*My Hero*

# 2

## WHAT HAPPENED BEFORE AND AFTER SCHOOL

*'One's dignity may be assaulted and vandalised, but it can never be taken away . . .'*
– Michael J Fox.

M y auntie's living room was fairly typical of council houses at the time, I suppose, with its odd, mismatched furniture, grey sofas and bright red floral carpet, part of which was protected by a clear plastic runner that made a sort of hallway area into the kitchen. There were lots of ornaments dotted around that house, and the windowsill was covered in plants and fake flowers. Under the window sat my cousin's green metal children's chair; I don't know why that sticks out, but it does.

GMTV was always on in the mornings, with Mr Motivator (my auntie's favourite), and then it was normally *Countdown* in the afternoons. These noisy programmes provided the backdrop to my time at my auntie's, and to this day, I'm taken back to that house whenever I hear them on the TV: I remember my sense of urgency as I'd try so hard to concentrate on the presenter's words. I'd push myself to find something to say, to participate in any way I could, knowing after a while what would happen if I couldn't . . .

I felt that way because there was a man that lived at my auntie's house. I thought of him as a sort of step-uncle at first, but the relationship was confusing to my six-year-old brain. To me, it looked as though they didn't do anything together at all; they ate different foods at different times (from different fridges), slept in separate rooms and essentially lived separate lives. I suppose he was no more than a lodger in my head.

I always knew when this man was around. You could smell the stale, old tobacco scent mixed in with the unmistakable musty smell of an ageing man whenever he was near. I couldn't get that smell off my own skin for years.

This man was monstrously tall to me, with an imposing beer belly, rough, red skin and a black moustache. I think he worked at a metal factory, but he wore suit trousers with dress shirts, ties and shiny black shoes all the time. There was little else remarkable about him, except to say he was an abuser – my abuser.

Memories are difficult to decipher sometimes. There are some things that stay with you, and it's difficult to pinpoint why, but they do. Just like the red knitted tank top this man wore over his fancy clothes, etched into my mind's eye, and the disgustingly too-long thumbnail that still haunts my dreams today.

This man stole my innocence. He assaulted my six-year-old body for his own pleasure, making me lookout (because there were always others around), confidant (bribing me to keep his secret) and black sheep of the family in the process.

The relentless abuse was mostly the same. He'd get what he wanted; I'd get on with my day. Sometimes, there'd be more members of the family at my auntie's, and we'd all be sitting around in the lounge watching *Countdown* or *Deal or No Deal* on TV and chatting when he'd subtly appear in the doorway. He'd try to catch my eye, and I'd fight to appear not to have noticed. Other times, I'd look before I realised I had, and he'd indicate I should follow him.

My auntie's kitchen was tiled in old council-mandated tiles, uninspiring and well-worn, with white cupboards surrounding the room, top and bottom. There was a door in that kitchen that led out into her garden, and by that back door, a green and yellow budgie sat watching from his cage, the subject of mine and my cousin's naïve, childlike torment back in the day. It wasn't a big space, but I won't forget it.

This man's fridge sat opposite my auntie's and was empty most of the time apart from housing his beer. But occasionally, Mom would go shopping to Birmingham city centre, and she'd bring him back a lobster or pheasant to go in that fridge. That really confused me; it felt at times that Mom would treat this man like a father figure, even going so far as to buy him Christmas presents (her own dad had died before I was born), and I saw no good reason for her to do that, especially as I don't think I ever saw him and my auntie even talk!

Back in that kitchen, when he had me where he wanted, this man would turn me around and bend me over, pulling my trousers and knickers over my trembling little bum and then he'd rape me until he was satisfied. Every thrust inside my tiny frame sent shockwaves of pain right into my tummy. I felt so sore; it hurt so much. Seconds felt like hours, but I learned quickly how to detach from reality to survive in the moment. No matter what I did, though, I just couldn't stop the feeling that I was getting dirtier and dirtier until he'd finally pull away.

Afterwards, I'd go to the bathroom and dry myself. I felt sticky, sore and shameful, but I did as I was told. When I'd come back, I'd get my bribe – £5 that eventually turned into £20. He said it was because I was a good girl; I didn't know what that meant, but I knew it was more than he was giving my cousin, and I knew it was more than I was ever going to get at home, with Mom then being a 28-year-old single mom to me and my brother until she met C. I felt somehow happy with this money, which only added to my confusion.

This man no doubt saw the vulnerability in me. I was six years old, and he preyed on my youthful naivety and trusting heart, but worse, he somehow recognised the endless cravings I had for the love and attention that I wasn't getting at home. It was this that he used to get close to me, by making me feel special, wanted, noticed . . .

This man manipulated me into submission and gaslighted me into silence while he raped my poor little body for seven long years, and the damage he caused was horrific.

I remember thinking a lot, while it was going on, about whether this was normal. After all, I didn't have a dad around in my house to see any difference. But I knew it didn't feel right; it hadn't from the start. I'd been left feeling dirty and disgusting every time, and nobody else had ever made me feel like that. Besides, I was told never to mention 'the game' we had played (so I hadn't), but if I couldn't mention it, did this mean it wasn't normal? Did other dads not do this?

And if not, if their kids didn't have to suffer this, then why did I? Why me?

*Nursery/ Reception (Elm Street)*

*Albion Road*

.

# 3

## A CRY FOR HELP, UNANSWERED

*'It's not the strongest of the species that survive, nor the most
intelligent, but the ones most responsive to change.'*
– Charles Darwin

I can't remember the age at which I stopped genuinely
smiling. Of course, I still forced a pose for the odd photo,
when it was needed, and I became good at acting the part
around others. But as for genuinely happy smiling, I really
didn't have a cause.

Although I progressed at school, I'd still suffer my abuser
when I was at my auntie's house. I became a jealous bully,
hating myself and the way I looked and almost needing to
inflict pain on myself and on others. Looking back, It was
obvious I needed control over something in my life, but I
was also acting out for attention; this was my cry for help.

Growing up with Mom, I'd obviously inherited a lot of

her values, but the most damaging was definitely the tired old notion that children should be seen and not heard, and that if I cried, I'd be given something to cry for: It was a raging battle in my brain to make sense of the world the grown-ups were weaving for me, with all its twists and turns, inconsistencies and hypocrisies.

In our family, we don't express our emotions either, which adds another level of discomfort to an already uncomfortable dynamic. This meant Mom was apparently oblivious to the nightmares I endured, despite my changing behaviour, which manifested in bullying, smoking weed and promiscuity.

I did break the family code at one point and told my brother, but he was just a kid and his response showed it - he thought it had been an accident. Then my cousin, J, who once walked in on him hurting me in my auntie's kitchen, didn't tell anyone as he didn't understand anything sexual at the time. But, he did tell his Mom, once when he turned 18 and back then, when we were around the age of seven, (for the both of us), that my abuser was showing us pornography on his tv and dirty magazines. I think there was a family meeting after this; I was told to keep away from him, he just got told off, and that was that.

One night, when Mom was first seeing her third partner after losing my dad, C, I was sent to stay over at my auntie's so the two of them could go out clubbing together. I didn't like C much at all, to begin with. I think I resented him coming into my family and getting so comfortable. And I made my dislike for him obvious; I reminded him on more than one occasion that he wasn't my dad.

The night they went out, you wouldn't believe the fear that gripped me or the adrenaline that coursed through my veins as I cried, begged and pleaded for them not to send me to my aunties. Now that I'm the adult, I can't imagine forcing a child, that desperate to not have to do something, into doing it, but somehow they did and I was sent away for the night.

That night, in that room, I lay awake in the dark, focusing on the sounds of the house, listening out for the smallest change that would mean he was coming. Feeling like helpless prey as I lay there trembling, I waited for the lion to come, and he did - of course, he did.

As I grew, Sex Education was introduced at school and I became very aware that I could fall pregnant. I had a few school friends come with me to The Hatherton Centre on a few occasions for the morning-after pill. At this point, I'd been able to (mostly), hide this dirty secret, but I panicked that I wouldn't be able to hide a baby. So I started to take the contraceptive pill, around the age of 11/12, which Mom then found in my bedroom. She wasn't happy, called me a slag and accused me of sleeping around the West Midlands!

During this period of my life, I'd grown closer to C's daughter, K, (C's child by another woman). I was six when Mom met C and K had been four, so we became close because of the small age gap. We bonded quickly, but we got up to no good, during this time in my life. We wagged school together and stayed out when we weren't supposed to. Mom seemed to resent our relationship, even going so far as to appear jealous at times of the bond that we shared.

Later on, even through the darker times, K and I remained close. In our early twenties, when we had boyfriends and had passed our driving tests, we'd just go driving and follow each other around. Until recently, I had the luxury of being able to drive past her house when I was out and about, and being able to spot her car. I'd think to myself, 'K's at work today', I'd have an idea of what she was up to. But, things aren't so good for K now; there's no car to spot on the driveway anymore.

Back in the day, not even when the police brought me home, time after time, (after I'd been out misbehaving), did the questions about whether I was ok, come. But, I wasn't so surprised by then, I'd already been fooling those around me about the money I'd been flashing around, (what else was I supposed to do with it?), telling them I was just really lucky at winning those foil wrapped prizes in bags of Walkers crisps, (which contained £20 or a free bag of crisps!).

I look back now and it's tough for me to understand how they bought all the lies: I really don't understand why my cries for help remained unheard until I finally found the strength to say the words they couldn't ignore.

*Christmas, opening presents with my little sis.*

# 4

## YEAR 2004

*'In the silence behind what can be heard, lies the answers we've been searching for, for so long.'*
–Andreas Fransson

'll never forget the details of that Bank Holiday Monday... Mom and I were already arguing about something. It was approximately mid-morning and we were probably arguing over me wanting to go out with friends and play, which wasn't unusual in our house. I was definitely in my bedroom, where I spent most of my days, (to be honest, I only really came downstairs when I ate my meals, as we'd stopped watching TV, soaps, or doing anything as a family ages ago, really).

Anyway, I remember Mom saying "... the devil ah ride you." Meaning she thought I was possessed, or that someone had really mashed up my brain, the way I was acting. And it was then that I said it: I said "Yeah, my abuser mashed up my brain."

We argued and I persisted; I'd said it now, I wasn't going to stop. I said his name loud and clear, more than a few times, in absolute tears. I was sobbing that he abused me. Mom came into my room, from her's, where she'd been shouting from, and she did what I call that old Jamaican laugh, "Hey heyyy, you best be telling the truth because a whole lot of people you going to hurt, like E, (her taxi driver friend), as it's his people and you best be telling the truth. Them would have to bring him back from Jamaica!"

She went on and on, but I think she was mainly in shock at that point. I have to believe that because she also said it was my own fault for being too nice to people. She told me, "... we told you to stay away from him." which I recognised was her way of passing on the blame, rather than accepting the awful truth. But then it got worse when she started throwing my things out of the window. I remember a handful of school friends walking past during all of this: V, M, perhaps D and C. I was so embarrassed that my underwear was all over the front lawn, I felt the (by now), familiar waves of shame washing over me again.

I'd messaged my boyfriend at the time, M, in a blind panic as it was a bank holiday, meaning there'd be no public transport round by us, and it was more than clear I'd be leaving my family home today. M had gone to his Mom, who arrived soon after, to pick me up in a lime-green people carrier. I can still see her looking at me now, it was utter shock. She must've thought Mom had lost the plot!

To be fair, my Mom, that day, looked the angriest I'd ever seen her, the angriest she'd ever been in her life, as we drove away with just the clothes I was wearing. I'll never forget the way she looked as we left, but what was worse was the apathy when the police returned me later on to get my stuff. I was 13 and it was all just routine, no warnings over breaking the law by kicking your underage child out onto the streets, no remorse or takebacks; I collected my things and didn't look back.

Back then, I didn't know what to say, but as an adult, I wrote a letter to my Mom…

*Dear Mom, (Mother Goose),*

*I lost a part of me that shouldn't have gone so soon; my childhood was taken from me.*

*But Mom, you were the first person to break my heart, when it should have been someone else, you should've been helping to pick up the pieces instead. I hate not knowing if I want you in my life or not.*

*The lessons I've learned from you are not to trust people and to always be strong and so everyday is a battle between my head and my heart as to whether to have you there, or not. I won't just watch you make the same mistakes with your grandchild, that's a risk I'm not willing to take.*

*I know we will never have the closeness we both might want, I feel like I've tried too many times. So many times in my life have I come to you for guidance, but I feel as if I get nothing back.*

*I want you to know that I grew into this resilient person, who can now brush the water off her back, but only because there were times where I would have drowned holding onto useless emotions that came so close to taking me under.*

*Through all the pain, despite everything that has happened, you should know that I will be ok. But I have to let go now; it's time!*

*Kind regards*
*Janet*

# 5

## FALSE START

*'Dances without purpose have false starts and stops.'*
–Hanya Holm

uckily, M's family had offered me a place to go to when I needed it and at the same time, I began to spend more time with C, who was struggling to find his feet, having recently broken up with my Mom. C didn't have much, but what he did have, he shared with me, so I split my time between his flat and Ms family home. It was a new start for me.

Looking back, I can see the kind-hearted gestures that came my way during this time from C, were just that, but in those moments, I was still very firmly engaged in survival mode. C would put his arm around me and I'd throw it straight off - we didn't do cuddles in our family! We clashed again and again, because I was always out, but, admittedly, my memory fails me around this time, as I catapulted head-first and far too young into the adult world: A lot of it is a blur.

Eventually, my things ended up on M's doorstep and his parents took me in, until I could go into a hostel at 16 years old, in three years' time. That didn't go quite to plan, though, as we fell in love, my first love, and so we moved into a place together, a HMO where we thought we were free and could live our lives the way we wanted.

Days turned into weeks and our only focus was each other. The problem was, I was still craving love and security, while trying to make sense of my past. You could almost claim that was my ambition, to find that unconditional love, a love that came without strings attached, and I thought I'd found it with M. But as the weeks rolled into months, things started to fall apart.

It didn't take long for me to learn that alcohol numbed the pain. It took me far enough out of my inner turmoil that I could be like the others around me, who all seemed so carefree and innocent. Alcohol became my friend and my medicine, but in time, it became my illness and it almost became my undoing.

M smoked a lot of weed and I drank a lot of alcohol. On the face of it, I just wanted to go out and party, be young, hedonistic and live it up! M was more comfortable staying in the house and smoking. I think he was an introvert and despite my experiences growing up, I wanted to get out into the world; at that time, our paths just wouldn't align.

Around the age of 17, we moved into an apartment in West Bromwich on our own. By that point, M had a pretty serious cannabis habit and was becoming increasingly more physically aggressive; the more he couldn't get his fix, the worse his behaviour would get. I tried to avoid the stark reality of my situation by partying hard and soon our lives together began to fall apart.

In time, our relationship was more physical attraction than love. We inevitably split up and he had gone back to his parents' house, while I moved to nearby Tipton and began working at a care home called Dovedale Court. There, I met a lad who was half Italian and half African, his name was Rico. We soon started seeing each other, but I quickly found out he was also very controlling and before long he had caused me to get mixed up in fraud and into a lot of debt.

Rico and I argued a lot when money was low, and I was the only source of income working at the care home, so money was low a lot of the time. To make matters worse, his behaviour led me to believe he was cheating at the time and it didn't take too long before I'd just had enough. I remember, at one point, I called my brother to come and help me to escape from this toxic relationship, but no one knew where I lived by then, after all, it had been nearly 5 years since anyone had seen me in person, and for all I knew, they didn't know if I was dead or alive.

Seeing no way out, I attempted an overdose then: I

had locked the ensuite bathroom door and taken as many Paracetamol tablets as I could. I don't remember the exact details of what happened next, but I know that Rico kicked the bathroom door off and called an Ambulance. I remember being blue-lighted to Sandwell Hospital, but everything else was a blur. Once there, I had my stomach pumped and was made to drink a black charcoal liquid, then the hospital kept me in overnight, where I was monitored.

This wasn't a cry for help, this was me having had enough of everything I had gone through, with no one by my side.

# 6

## HARM AND HEALTH

*'Health is like money, we never have a true idea of its*
*value until we lose it.'*
– Josh Billings

In 2009, I was 18 years old and I was in the hospital, having just had my stomach pumped. I know someone called Mom and told her I was there, but she didn't come, for whatever reason. Only C visited me at the hospital.

The hospital staff all did their jobs well, and so they could tell I was scared of Rico. They asked me lots of questions around domestic abuse and I remember there was some sort of meeting with a drug and alcohol counsellor/ domestic violence advisor, but I was just one of a number of patients needing help and so, unsurprisingly, I left not much better than I went in and that was back home to Rico.

When things didn't get any better, I somehow managed

to move on and I met G three years later, around the age of 21. I really felt he was my soulmate - we even planned to marry!

G worked hard as a car washer, at different garages, throughout our entire relationship, as did his family. I remember meeting him on that first night at WS1, a club in Walsall. I thought he was just my type until he spoke and I knew the language barrier (he being Romanian), would make it difficult for us to pursue a relationship with each other, but somehow we did. We used Google Translate for a while until G could speak good enough English to get by.

G must have been around 19 or 20 when we first got together. We lived together in Tipton for 4 or 5 years, but life wasn't easy. G and his family, despite already being here, all needed the correct documents to enable them to legally work in the UK as foreign nationals. This meant they had to take whatever work they could get, they didn't always have paid work, and they couldn't always afford to eat. In time, I felt that our relationship wasn't just the two of us anymore, I felt responsible for everyone, even going so far as to take short-term live-in carer jobs so I could pay for us all to eat.

I had bigger worries after a time though. I started to feel ill, gradually. I'd bend down to pick something up and my vision would become blurry, and I'd find myself getting dizzy more and more. Soon a doctor confirmed I had a tumour that was pressing against my brain; I'd need treatment for the next 12 months to shrink it. It was a prolactinoma tumour in my pituitary gland, which risked my fertility and long-term vision if left untreated. I was terrified, but I was glad to have G by my side.

Then, one night in 2012, I was feeling ok, so I went to my next-door neighbour's where we would drink on a Friday after I finished work. It was a quiet one. At some point, I suggested a game of Monopoly, and I remember it being a laugh, but before long I'd passed out drunk on the sofa.

When I woke, it was to find out I'd been assaulted and raped while I lay there. I didn't tell anyone right away, but I was so scared I climbed out of my neighbour's living room window and went back to my flat, where I ran a bath, before getting into bed with G. I told G at the dinner table around lunchtime, the next day. He reacted instantly, smashed his dinner plate against the wall and went downstairs to the neighbours where he explained what had gone on. The rapist had been there, but escaped through the back door and left.

I went to the police station at West Brom with my friend K. I remember standing at the front desk and whispering to the officer that I had been raped. They called me through and questioned me thoroughly. There were numerous questions, some of them leaving me feeling like I was the perpetrator at the time. There were also questions like 'had I had a wash afterwards?' And I felt violated again with another rape kit. Afterwards, I was sent home in paper underwear, alone.

As if the event wasn't bad enough, I started to get notes pushed through the letterbox soon after my assault, and one day a DVD with the writing 'Dream Believer' on it, fell onto the doormat. I told the police about the DVD and they said it was a quote and it was meant to accuse me of lying. Thankfully, that was as bad as it got in terms of harassment. But the fallout from that night didn't end there.

Despite his initial reaction, G thought I'd cheated, until my case went to Wolverhampton Crown court, in 2013, where the truth of that night was laid bare. No one was there for me at that time. I had told Mom and some others about the rape, but I had no support with this and went to court with a rape counsellor from Black Country Women's Aid. Our relationship was already breaking under the strain of our daily living circumstances, but this had been the final nail in the coffin for G and me. I'd already resumed drinking to numb the pain and we had long stopped sharing a bed.

When G attended court, I felt a flicker of hope, but It was too late to go back though, his lack of trust in me hurt more than he'll ever know. But, even worse, was the return of the old, familiar feeling of my cries for help going unheard. I needed him to support me, but his lack of trust damaged what we had beyond all repair. I drank around three bottles of wine every day to forget and the weight just dropped off me.

Loneliness became my only companion.

It's not surprising that I ended up being arrested in

2013. My drinking was out of control and there was no one around to tell me to stop or to show me what I was doing to myself.

*Should of got Married 24th November 2013.*

# 7

## COPING AND CONTROL

*'She was never prepared for all the shit she went through, but she
got through it. She always will.'*
– Abby Rose

I developed coping mechanisms that allowed me to put one
foot in front of the other and try to live my life. Then
I met Sergeant L late in 2013 on a dating website and
really felt like this was the chance I needed to straighten my
life out. He was clever and confident and I fell for it all. I
waited for a year to start a life with this man, as he served
in Afghanistan and when that year was up, I flew with high
hopes to be with him in Germany.

I didn't know anyone or anything in Germany, but I
wasn't worried because my sergeant would be waiting for
me. What I also didn't know then, was that he was very
much still married and had three children too. He promised

me he'd get a divorce and I believed him, but soon his real personality reared its ugly head and his other family was the least of my problems.

I gave my trust to Sergeant L, and, as had happened in my past, it was horrifically abused. We'd argue, as couples do, but he would lose his temper frighteningly. It wasn't uncommon for him to strangle me until I passed out. One day, I woke with an enormous lump on my head, roughly the size of a tennis ball. I didn't know what had happened to me, but he told me I'd fallen down while drunk. I looked around the room and could tell instantly we'd had a scuffle; there were nail varnish marks smudged against the wall. And I knew just what could have caused that lump on my head, as I spotted his steel-toe-cap boots across the room.

By that time, Sergeant L had taken my passport off me, rendering me a prisoner in a foreign country, and after the lump appeared on my head, he locked me in the barracks and went off for some mesh meeting. I managed to contact someone I knew from school who was also serving in the army. They came and got me out and helped me try to get help. The trouble was, as I wasn't a military wife, the military hospital wouldn't see me and I didn't know what else to do, so I went back.

Sergeant L continued to manipulate me and soon after the last incident, we ended up on a trip to Egypt. Sergeant L attacked me for the last time while we were there, throwing my phone down the toilet. I realised no one would know if

I was dead or alive; I could literally disappear and no one would be any the wiser. I had to make a change.

A week later, I gathered the courage, took back my passport and ran home to the UK. Where I desperately sought medical attention for my horrific head injury. He followed me and gave me the same old sob story, the one where he'd change and life would be so good. Instead, he flew back to Germany, before leaving to serve in Canada for six months, having put a tracking device on me so he could remain in control.

My life was anything but mine, I'd come to realise. Time after time, I'd given my trust openly and I'd been hurt so often. People had come into my life, taken what they wanted and now a psychopath pulled my strings. I knew that if didn't stop things here, he was more than capable of killing me, and if not him, then someone else might just step into that place.

I made up my mind that this was the moment my life would change. And, despite still struggling to control my alcohol intake, and a second arrest in 2016, (I was placed on an Alcohol Awareness program at The Beacon in Walsall, where Early Help also got involved over concerns over my drinking), it did!

*Messages from Sergeant L*

*Message-exchange between myself and Sergeant L while in Germany barracks.*

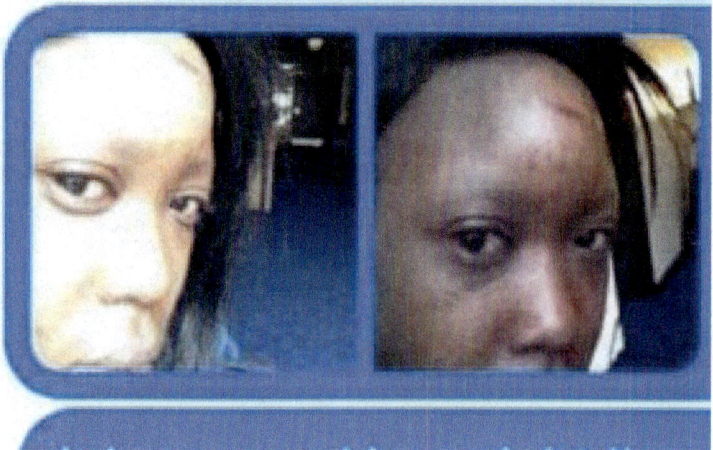

*Calling for help from soldiers I knew.*

# 8

## ALL FOR ESMÉ

*'There is no freedom waiting for you on the breeze of the sky, and you ask, "what if I fall?" Oh, but my darling. What if you fly?'*
— Erin Hanson

I finally had the space and time to breathe. Sergeant L would be in Canada for six months, over 1100 miles away: We were thankfully separated by seas and now, I could stop looking over my shoulder for a while.

I stepped out of the shadows and into the world again and in no time at all, I met someone new. I fell pregnant quickly and didn't know what to do at first. I decided to tell Sergeant L, who wanted me to tell my new partner that I'd had an abortion, so we could raise the baby together, but I was scared; I'd planned on making the break from him for a reason.

Desperately seeking help, I called a domestic violence

helpline and told them of my situation and of his threats; I told them of the pictures of bullets he would send to me. The charity called in Social Services, who became involved and soon told me I would be placing my baby in danger if I went back to Sergeant L. I'd already realised if he could harm me the way he had been, he could be capable of doing harm to a child that wasn't his and I wasn't going to let that happen.

So, when I was just six weeks pregnant, I left them both and decided to start afresh, just me and my baby. It wasn't an easy decision; I was pregnant by a man I barely knew, had a psychotic boyfriend and I just didn't know if I could do this on my own. But, I did know my baby needed commitment, love and stability and I wasn't prepared for anyone to jeopardise that. I'd seen so many failures to provide and protect children, in the community around me and I wasn't sure I was capable of being any different, but I did know I'd spend the rest of our lives trying. Around that time, I was in contact with Mom and she advised me to keep my baby, (it was the best advice I ever had), and so I got on with life, as you do.

Now, my baby wasn't due yet, so I wasn't too concerned when I first noticed trickles of water in my underwear, around my 32nd week of pregnancy. But when I kept losing more, slowly, over a period of a couple of days, I knew she wasn't going to wait for long: And then it happened!

Luckily, I was at home when my waters broke spectacularly

and my best mate Jess was with me within 15 minutes. I called Mom too, but her response left me cold; she had shopping to be done. I had no birth plan, no family by my side, no partner and nowhere else to turn. As the tears came, my sister and step-sister arrived and packed my bag while I paced and leaked; Mom must have told them.

Somehow, I managed to get dressed and then I drove myself and Jess to the hospital and parked too far away to avoid the unaffordable parking fees. I was jabbed, tagged and given an internal examination by a male nurse, before being sent up to a ward on high security, in case Sergeant L turned up. He didn't, but it did shock me when my Romanian ex-boyfriend turned up to make sure we were ok. Shortly afterwards, Jess was sent home and I found myself alone again.

At 2 a.m. I was gripped with pain, but advised to go to sleep. My baby had other ideas though, and by 5 a.m. I was 5 centimetres dilated - there was no going back! My sister came around 6:15 a.m. with the news that Mom had to go to work. My heart sank, but then she appeared. I was overwhelmed, Mom was here, by my side, holding my hand, supporting me and my sister was here too: I felt surrounded by love as I pushed and cried.

Esmé was born at 7:04 a.m. in June 2015, seven weeks before her due date. I was in awe of her, but I could only hold her for the shortest time, as she had to go to the neonatal unit where she'd spend the first 12 days of her life.

Then, when she was strong enough to feed from the bottle, at 33 and a half weeks, Esmé was discharged and I took her home.

This should have been the most magical time for me, becoming a mother, but two months in, postnatal depression crept into our lives and took hold. In desperation to escape my feelings, I returned to the embrace of the bottle and fell into a familiarly depressing pattern. I'd wake each day and do everything a good Mom should; my baby was well-fed, clean and well looked after, but then she'd go to bed.

I'd drink at night, and that's the only thing I'd do. I wouldn't drink until I passed out, but it was enough to distract me from my lonely reality and the horrors of my past. When I told her about the depression, Mom told me to 'shake it off', and my brother told me to 'told me to lie in the bed I had made'; it was the attitude of the time, but it didn't help one bit! And so I soon stopped bothering with how I looked, ignored my own pain, stopped eating if I didn't have to and lurched from day to day on autopilot. I felt I couldn't ask for help: I just held on for Esmé.

As she grew, I fed off the progress she made from the first time she called me Mom and the times she crawled, cruised and took those first few steps. I know I will forever be her protector, her Mom and her dad: I will never let my baby girl down.

For me, it's almost like reliving my childhood all over again, but this time it's for the both of us and I'm determined to get it right! I commit to giving Esmé not just the materialistic things that she will ever need, but all the true love a child deserves and the one thing that you can't get back if you don't give it the first time around, and that's time!

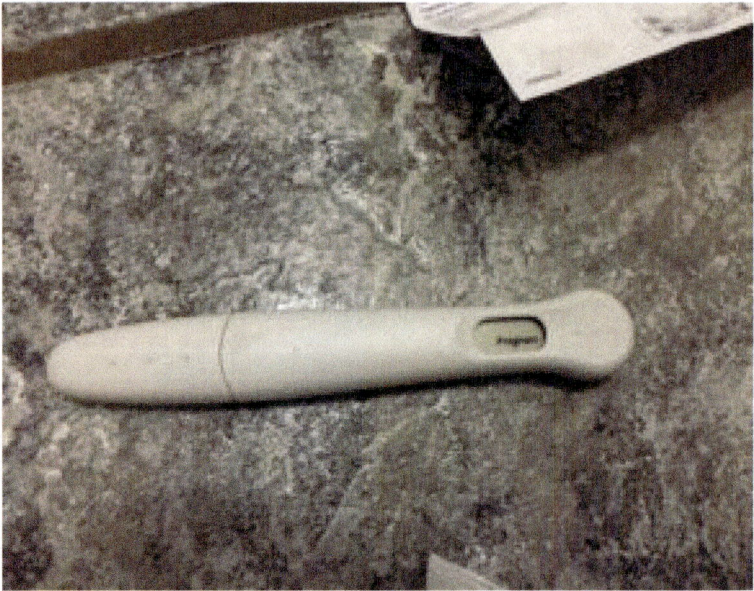

*Finding out I was pregnant*

*2 months before giving birth*

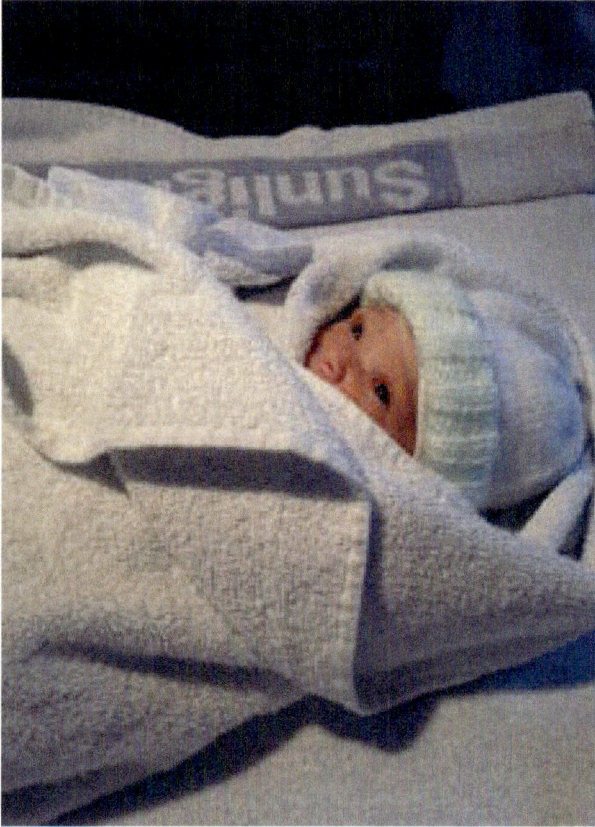

*Seconds of her being born.*

*2 days after Esmé was born. My birthday.*

*Being told she needs skin 2 skin on my hospital visits*

*Hospital Visits*

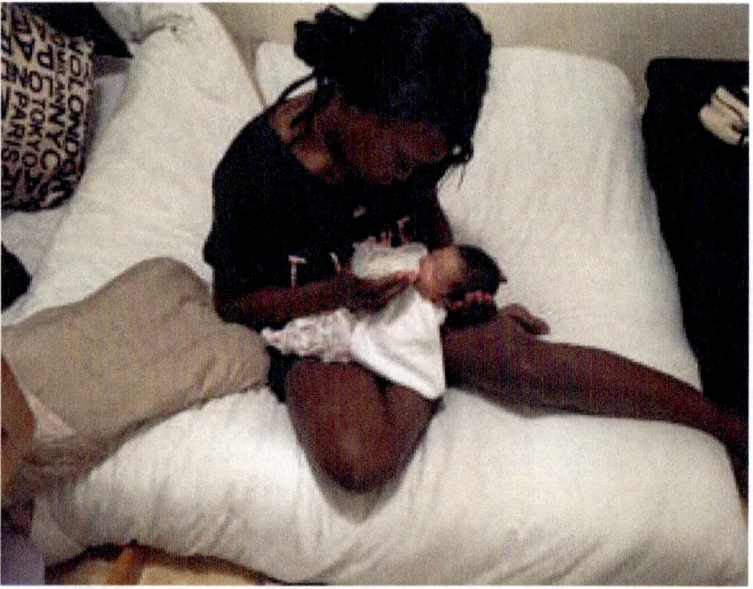

*First time bringing her home, the struggles, when times I couldn't afford a bed.*

*1st Birthday Cake Smash*

*#Besties #CBeebies #3rdBirthdaytreat*

*Disneyland*

*#Besties #CBeebies #3rdBirthdaytreat*

*Disneyland Paris*

# 9

## LOOKING FORWARD

*'What matters in life is not what happens to you but
how you tell the story.'*
– The Connor Brothers

In February 2017, I somehow found the strength I needed
and reached out to a drink addiction programme and the
Early Help and Family Support Teams in my community.
I'd grown to realise my behaviour was going to have an
impact on my parenting if I carried on this way. The team
was great; they supported me through my battle with
alcoholism, with my mental health needs, and they ensured
I continued to safeguard and provide well for my daughter.
Around the same time, I took a leap of faith and found
enough inner strength and self-belief to apply for an online
course in counselling studies, and I was even granted a letter
of support from my family support worker confirming my

efforts to be a better parent and dedication to turning my life around.

I thought my journey might have been easier, but because of my lack of formal qualifications from school and my arrest for abusing police officers, I had to battle for recognition from the BACP. Eventually, though, I was taken seriously, and I enrolled first as a college student at Wolverhampton College in 2017 and then at Staffordshire University, in September 2020 and now I'm studying for a master's degree in Psychology at Wolverhampton University. Little did I know, that I would benefit so much!

My counselling studies encouraged me to rediscover my identity, but this involved unravelling my past, and it's here, now I'm qualified, registered and have counselled over 1,000 clients across four platforms that I find myself ready to share my story and make my contribution to raising awareness of the signs of early childhood abuse and neglect and the effects of inaction. Now, I am fortunate in that I can work hard to make a difference in mainstream and sanction schools, working with pupils who have suffered abuse, gun crime, knife crime and so much more.

I know now what unconditional love is. Esmé taught me that, and I will strive for the rest of my life to make sure she never knows anything else. It's for her that I rise each day and work hard, and it's for her that I want to make a change in the world, one where children are heard as much as they are seen.

But there's something else inside me that remains unsatisfied, and I think I'll always feel that way because while I do reach out to others, through my work and in my spare time using social media, I know there are so many unheard voices in the world, voices that need, no, *deserve* to be heard.

I know how much of an impact not being heard has had on my life. From those dirty secrets, trapped inside an uncomprehending mind causing anger and frustration, that spilled over into the lives of those around me, to acting out, in my case to the extent that it wasn't unheard of for the police to be my ride home, I've struggled with my own self-relationship, and I've struggled with relationships with others, unsurprisingly. Now, I'm a stronger person, but it hasn't been easy.

The facts are undeniable: one in five adults between the ages of 18 and 74 have experienced a form of abuse in childhood (before age 16) – **one in five!** The estimated figure of adult survivors of child sexual abuse is a staggering 3.1 million, but given the themes within my story, it's not outlandish to consider that figure to be wildly conservative. In fact, one in seven adult callers that reached out to the National Association for People Abused in Childhood had not told anybody before that call: depressingly, this translates as an estimated one in eight victims never coming to the attention of statutory authorities. In reality, this means children are often stuck in abuse cycles, and adults often turn to unhealthy or self-destructive behaviours to cope with the nightmares.

We need to break the walls of silence down. For far too long, children have been scapegoats for the inadequacies (the uncertainty, the embarrassment, the awkwardness in facing difficult truths) of the adults around them, and it's devastating to that child's life. We need to talk!

In writing this book, I am inching closer to having a form of closure, one that will enable me to enjoy the rest of my life without shame. But, in publishing, I have two objectives I'd like to achieve:

- To raise awareness of one story, of the signs that children are silently screaming in your world and to implore you to act;
- To encourage and empower others (or you?) who've suffered similar experiences to speak up.

In looking forward to the rest of my life, I have an abundance of ideas and definitely no shortage of passion for seeing my goals through. Already through my work, I am assisting others in coming to terms with experiences that have adversely affected them, and in my private life, I have developed a Facebook group and Instagram page (details at the back of this book) in the hopes of building a community of support and mutual growth.

In the future, I will be expanding these efforts and

further plan to write more books concentrating on different aspects of my story and providing support, information and guidance for speaking up, stepping in and reducing those secretive walls to rubble. Watch this space.

And when she's older, Esmé will know how much I have fought to change the world for her and for the billions of other children who might've faced what I faced.

And she will know I did so much more than survive!

My message to my readers, to you, is this... There is a light at the end of the tunnel, so don't give up on yourself, no matter what. Believe in you: That's all that matters!

Join me in:

- Empathising with other people
- Taking steps to reduce stress
- Being proud, but still reaching out and speaking up to others
- Becoming self-motivated
- Inspiring others
- Empowering others to take control of their own personal journey
- Helping others to come forward; standing tall and speaking out
- Putting out good into the world and reaping the rewards as it returns to you
- Leaving your comfort zone
- Understanding that it's ok to falter

- Changing the inside, and the outside falls into place
- Believing you are a star!

I want the world to know that whenever there's no hope, you can look up for that brightest star in the sky and that'll be me, and you, and all of us, guiding each other, reminding ourselves that we are no longer alone and we can all shine bright!

**Janet Linton**
MA, Bsc

⭐⭐⭐⭐⭐

✓ Verified Credentials    ✓ I'm Featured!

👤 About Me                                    ⌃

I specialise in person-centred counselling
which means I work with my clients in a
client-led, non-directive way. This allows
me to help you dig deeper into your
feelings to find clarity and/or give you
closure that you need, thus enabling me
not to teach you but rather allows us to
explore and manage the emotions you are
feeling.

As a creative therapist/counsellor I like to
gain the tr[       GET STARTED       ]ding a
quality servic................pport

*Online Therapy*

# Janet Linton

**bacp** | Registered Member
381560
MBACP

Registered Member MBACP

*BACP*

## Survivors of D&R

677 likes · 684 followers

Promote

See dashboard

Add to Story

Posts    About    Photos ▾    Mentions

Home    Watch    Page    Feeds    Notifications    Menu

*Survivors of D&R (business page) - Facebook*

*Survivors of Domestic & Rape (private page) - Facebook*

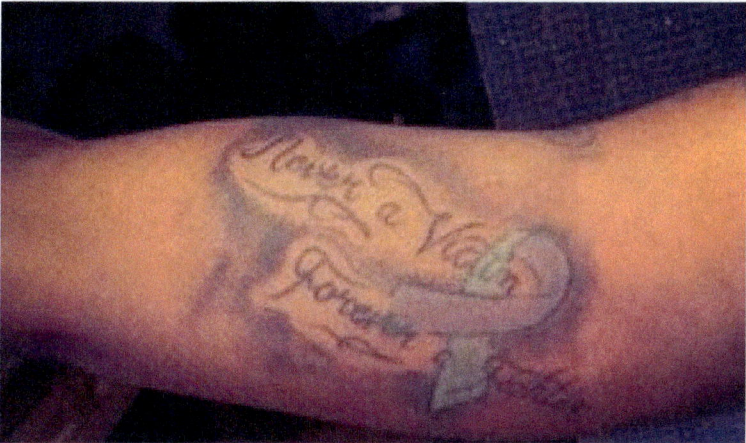

*Domestic abuse and Child abuse Ribbon (My Tattoo)- Never a Victim, Forever a Fighter*

*Staffordshire University Graduation*

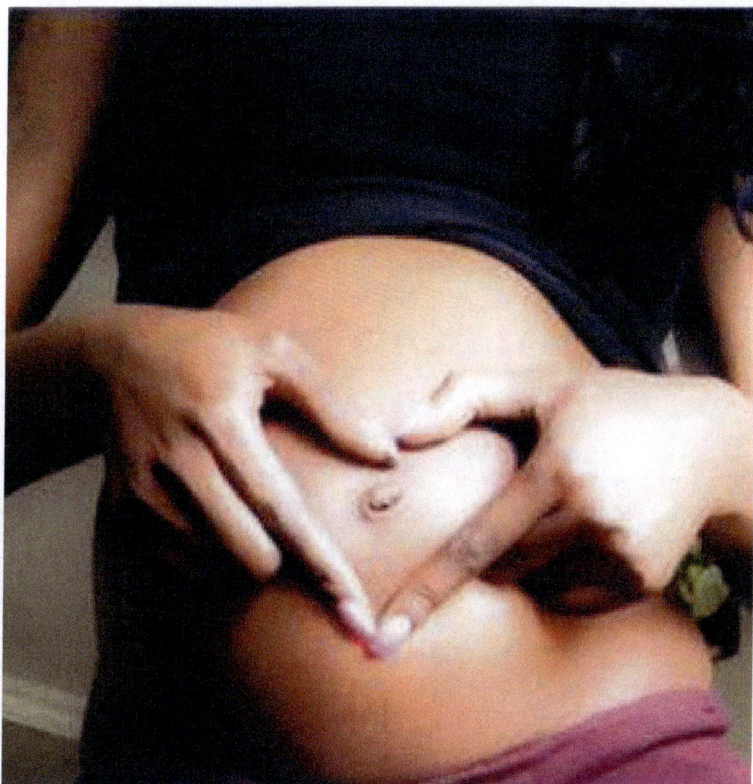

# ACKNOWLEDGEMENTS

*I want to say a massive thank you to my beautiful daughter Esmé for keeping my soul alive and showing me what unconditional love is.*

*Thank you to StoryTerrace, my writer Sarah R, my editor Sandra R and my artist Stephanie R, for creating my book cover.*

*Lastly thank you to my readers for trusting & believing in me.*

*Janet*

*A note from the ghost writer…*

*It's not often you come across an extraordinary story, with a leading lady that is so full of life and love and who has so much to give. This describes Janet, who I only had the pleasure of meeting to produce this book, but who has left an indelible mark upon my own psyche forever.*

*Janet's story is an inspirational one. It begins under a dark cloud and gathers momentum, threatening the most ferocious of storms coming her way, but what makes Janet so special, is how she stands tall, reaches up into those clouds and breaks them apart. Ray by ray, the sunlight floods through the gaps and lights up. Janet's story as we head towards her conclusion, but this won't be all from Janet, I have a feeling from this lady, there is an awful lot more to come!*

*Sarah R.*

StoryTerrace

Printed in Great Britain
by Amazon